Becker Professional Education, a global leader in professional education, has beer ACCA for more than 20 years, and thousands of candidates studying for the ACC their professional examinations through its Platinum and Gold ALP training center: and Central Asia.*

Becker Professional Education has also been awarded ACCA Approved Content Provider Status for materials for the Diploma in International Financial Reporting (DipIFR).

Nearly half a million professionals have advanced their careers through Becker Professional Education's courses. Throughout its more than 50-year history, Becker has earned a strong track record of student success through world-class teaching, curriculum and learning tools.

We provide a single destination for individuals and companies in need of global accounting certifications and continuing professional education.

*Platinum – Moscow, Russia and Kiev, Ukraine. Gold – Almaty, Kazakhstan

Becker Professional Education's ACCA Study Materials

All of Becker's materials are authored by experienced ACCA lecturers and are used in the delivery of classroom courses.

Study Text: Gives complete coverage of the syllabus with a focus on learning outcomes. It is designed to be used both as a reference text and as part of integrated study. It also includes the ACCA Syllabus and Study Guide, exam advice and commentaries and a Study Question Bank containing practice questions relating to each topic covered.

Revision Question Bank: Exam style and standard questions together with comprehensive answers to support and prepare students for their exams. The Revision Question Bank also includes past examination questions (updated where relevant), model answers and alternative solutions and tutorial notes.

Revision Essentials Handbook*: A condensed, easy-to-use aid to revision containing essential technical content and exam guidance.

*Revision Essentials Handbook are substantially derived from content reviewed by ACCA's examining team.

Substantially derived from content reviewed by ACCA's examining team

ACCA

PAPER F5

PERFORMANCE MANAGEMENT

OBJECTIVE TEST QUESTION PRACTICE

For Computer Based Examinations to June 2017

This training material has been prepared and published by Becker Professional Development International Limited:

Parkshot House
5 Kew Road
Richmond
Surrey
TW9 2PR
United Kingdom

ISBN: 978-1-78566-362-8

Acknowledgement

Past ACCA examination questions are the copyright of the Association of Chartered Certified Accountants and have been reproduced by kind permission.

CONTENTS

This supplement includes OT question types that will appear **only** in a computer-based exam, but provides valuable practice for all students whichever version of the exam they are sitting.

ACCA's CBE Specimen will be accessible from the exam resource finder
http://www.accaglobal.com/uk/en/student/exam-support-resources.html

Introduction

"Multiple choice – single answer" – is the standard OT type in paper-based examinations. In CBE this type is presented with radio bullets instead of A B, C, D options.

Illustration

Cim Co has two divisions, A and B. Each division is currently considering the following separate projects:

	Division A	*Division B*
Capital required for the project	$32·6 million	$22·2 million
Sales generated by project	$14·4 million	$8·8 million
Operating profit margin	30%	24%
Cost of capital	10%	10%
Current return on investment of division	15%	9%

If residual income is used as the basis for the investment decision, which Division(s) would choose to invest in the project?

○　　　　Division A only
○　　　　Division B only
○　　　　Both Division A and Division B
○　　　　Neither Division A nor Division B

How to answer?

✓　Click on a radio button to select an answer from the choices provided.

✓　You can select only one.

✓　If you want to change your answer, click on your new choice and the original choice will be removed automatically.

Answer

- Division A only

  Division A: Profit = $14·4m × 30% = $4·32m
  Imputed interest charge = $32·6m × 10% = $3·26m
  Residual income = $1·06m

  Division B: Profit = $8·8m × 24% = $2·112m
  Imputed interest charge = $22·2m × 10% = $2·22m
  Residual income = $(0·108)m

OTHER OT TYPES

The following OT types appear **only** in CBE:

(1)　Multiple response
(2)　Pull down list
(3)　Number entry
(4)　Hot area
(5)　Hot spot
(6)　Enhanced matching

These are illustrated below.

(1) Multiple response

Description – candidates are required to select more than one response from the options provided by clicking the appropriate tick boxes.

Illustration 1

Which TWO of the following statements concerning the use of variable cost plus pricing are true?

☐ It is useful for short term pricing decisions

☐ It is useful in a perfectly competitive market

☐ The price may not cover all the fixed costs

☐ It ensures that profit is maximised

☐ It is most useful when fixed costs are high

How to answer?

✓ Two is the maximum you will be able to select.

✓ You can deselect a chosen answer to clear it.

✓ When you have chosen the required number, deselecting an answer will allow you to select another answer.

✓ Remember that to earn the 2 marks you must answer the whole question correctly; there are no partial marks.

Answer

☑ It is useful for short term pricing decisions

☑ The price may not cover all the fixed costs

(2) Pull down list

Description – candidates are required to select one answer from a list of choices in a drop down list.

Illustration 2

Brick by Brick (BBB) provides a range of building services, including garage conversions.

BBB has a policy to price all jobs at budgeted total cost plus 50%. Budgeted overheads for the year are $400,000 and these are currently absorbed on a labour hour basis. The total budgeted labour hours for the year is 40,000.

A typical garage conversion costs $3,500 in materials and takes 300 labour hours to complete. It requires only one site visit by a supervisor and needs only one planning document to be raised. In all cases, labour is paid $15 per hour.

What is the current price for a typical garage conversion using the current method of absorbing overheads?

Select...   ▼
$11,000
$14,700
$16,500
$22,000

How to answer?

✓ Select one answer from the pull down list.

✓ You can change your answer by selecting another option.

✓ Remember this is really no different to a traditional MCQ except that the list could have more than four options.

Answer

Price per unit using absorption cost plus 50%:

	$
Materials	3,500
Labour (300 × 15)	4,500
Overheads (300 ×10 (W))	3,000
Total cost	11,000
Plus mark-up (50%)	5,500
Current price	16,500

WORKING

Total overheads ÷ total labour hours = $400,000 ÷ 40,000 = $10 per labour hour.

(3)   Number entry

Description – candidates are required to key in a numerical response.

Illustration 3

XYZ operates a chain of 10 convenience stores. The directors are considering investing in a new system of Electronic Point of Sale (EPOS) cash registers with communication links to head office. The costs of the new system have been estimated as follows:

Capital costs	$
25 new EPOS cash registers @ $300	7,000
1 new server at head office	2,000
Software licenses	3,000
Data file setup costs	2,000
Staff training	2,000
	16,000

Operating costs per year	
Broadband internet connections	3,600
Software maintenance costs	500
	4,100

As a result of the project, the cost of renting the existing cash registers, totalling $2,000 per year will be saved. The purchasing manager believes that better information about sales and inventory levels will increase the volume of sales. He has estimated that annual contribution will increase by $20,300 each year. The system will last for five years, after which it will be replaced.

Ignoring inflation and the cost of capital, what would be the total net benefit of the new system over its five year life?

$ [   ]

How to answer?

✓ Enter a numerical value in the answer box. Pay attention to any instruction about how the answer should be rounded (e.g. "to the nearest $").

✓ The **only** permitted characters for numerical answer are:

   ❑ One full stop as a decimal point (if required);
   ❑ One minus symbol at the front of the figure if the answer is negative.

   For example: -10234.35

✗ No other characters, including commas, are accepted.

✓ You can change your answer by adding permitted characters or deleting one or more highlighted characters.

Answer

		$
1	*Annual benefits*	
	Increased annual contribution	20,300
	Renting of existing cash registers	2,000
	Annual operating costs	
	Broadband	(3,600)
	Maintenance costs	(500)
	Net annual benefits	18,200
	× 5 years 91,000	
	Less capital costs	(16,000)
	Net benefit	**75000**

(4) Hot area

Description – candidates are required to select one or more areas in an image as their answer(s).

Illustration 4

The following statements have been made about planning and control as described in the three tiers of Robert Anthony's decision-making hierarchy:

Strategic planning is concerned with making decisions about the efficient and effective use of existing resources	TRUE	FALSE
Operational control is about ensuring that specific tasks are carried out efficiently and effectively	TRUE	FALSE

How to answer?

✓ Click on a hotspot area to select an answer from the hotspot choices provided.

✓ You can select only one per line.

✓ The selected area will be highlighted.

✓ If you want to choose a different answer click on an alternative area.

✓ Remember that to earn the 2 marks you must answer the whole question correctly; there are no partial marks.

Answer

Strategic planning is concerned with making decisions about the efficient and effective use of existing resources		**FALSE**
Operational control is about ensuring that specific tasks are carried out efficiently and effectively	**TRUE**	

(5)   Hot spot

Description – candidates are required to select one or more points by clicking on an image.

Illustration 5

Click on the graph below to identify the value of Q at which profit will be maximised.

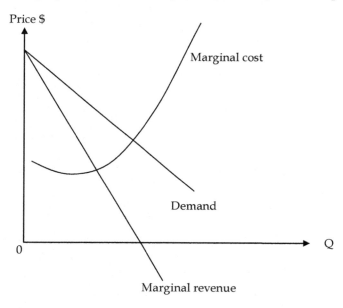

How to answer?

✓ Indicate your answer by click on the appropriate point in the graph.

✓ A dot will appear where you have clicked.

Answer

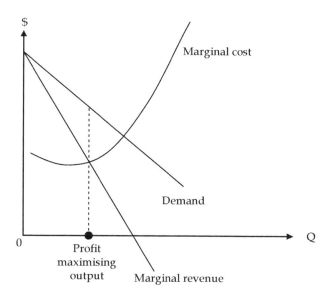

(6)   Enhanced matching

Description – candidates are required to select and drag their chosen answers to other areas of the screen.

Illustration 6

Different types of information systems provide the information which organisations need for strategic planning, management and operational control.

Match the following characteristic to the relevant information systems.

Characteristic
Facilitates the immediate processing of data
Reduces the opportunity for non-standard operations
Summarises internal data into periodic reports
Enables data to be easily shared between different departments
Usually includes data analysis and modelling tools
Can be set up with extranet links to customers and suppliers
Utilises dashboard facilities and interactive graphics
Supports structured decisions at the operational level

Management Information system	Transaction Processing System
MIS	TPS
MIS	TPS

Executive Information System	Enterprise Resource Planning System
EIS	ERPS
EIS	ERPS

How to answer?

✓ Select each characteristic from the left of the screen and drag it to the box representing the correct category.

✓ Answers can be moved to another category if you change your mind.

✓ Remember that to earn the 2 marks you must answer the whole question correctly; there are no partial marks.

Answer

Management Information System
Reduces the opportunity for non-standard operations
Summarises internal data into periodic reports

Executive Information System
Usually includes data analysis and modelling tools
Uses dashboard facilities and interactive graphics

Transaction Processing System
Facilitates the immediate processing of data
Supports structured decisions at the operational level

Enterprise Resource Planning System
Enables data to be easily shared between different departments
Can be set up with extranet links to customers and suppliers

OBJECTIVE TEST QUESTIONS

1   MULTIPLE RESPONSE

1.1   Which THREE of the following management accounting techniques might be used in environmental management accounting?

☐   Activity based costing

☐   Life-cycle costing

☐   Throughput accounting

☐   Input output analysis

1.2   A manufacturing company produces multiple products.

Which THREE of the following are required in order to calculate the break-even sales revenue for the company?

☐   The product mix ratio

☐   Contribution to sales ratio for each product

☐   General fixed costs

☐   Method of apportioning general fixed costs

☐   Budgeted sales of each product

1.3   Which TWO of the following measures could most suitably be used to assess the customer perspective of the balanced scorecard approach for an insurance company?

☐   New insurance products introduced in the period

☐   Training expenditure on sales representatives

☐   Average time to settle insurance claims

☐   Percentage of policy renewals

1.4   Tom Hopkin is responsible for managing the volume, quality and cost of production within his responsibility centre.

Which TWO of the following performance measures would be appropriate for measuring Tom's performance?

☐   Return on investment

☐   Materials usage variances

☐   Percentage of products that are defective after inspection

☐   Residual income

1.5   **Which THREE of the following statements about the return on investment method of performance measurement are true?**

☐   It enables comparison of performance of divisions which are not of common size

☐   Managers' decisions will be congruent with the goals of the organisation

☐   It does not take account of the risk of project investments being undertaken

☐   Managers will be encouraged to invest in projects with higher returns

☐   It is appropriate for a profit centre

1.6   Two divisions in an organisation have autonomy to decide whether to trade with each other or not, and to negotiate transfer prices. The selling division sells its output externally at the external market price.

In which TWO of the following situations would the selling division be prepared to sell internally for a transfer price that is below the external market price?

☐   Head office has imposed the transfer price

☐   The management of the selling division are seeking to restrict the quantity produced

☐   Some additional costs are incurred on external sales

☐   The selling division has some spare capacity after satisfying external demand for its output

1.7   **Which TWO of the following statements about expected values are true?**

☐   Expected value is of limited use for decisions regarding outcomes which will be repeated often

☐   Using expected value in decision-making can lead to the worst possible outcome being ignored

☐   The reliability of expected value calculations is heavily influenced by the accuracy of the probabilities assigned to outcomes

☐   Expected values take account of the risk associated with a decision

1.8   **Which TWO of the following does the manager have control over in a profit centre?**

☐   Generation of revenues

☐   Investment in non-current assets

☐   Investment in working capital

☐   Apportioned head office costs

☐   Depreciation

(16 marks)

2   PULL-DOWN LIST

2.1   Which costing approach identifies ways of making an acceptable profit margin on the market price of a product or service?

Select...   ▼
Activity-based costing
Benchmarking
Life-cycle costing
Target costing

2.2   Ardvec makes four products which sell in roughly equal volume. Data in respect of each product is shown below:

Per unit	Economy	Standard	Premium	Deluxe
Selling price	$28	$32	$37	$40
Variable cost	$13	$16	$20	$22
Direct labour hours	0·17	0·22	0·28	0·31

In the coming period, a shortage of direct labour means that Ardvec can only manufacture three products.

Which product should NOT be produced in order to maximise short-term profit?

Select...   ▼
Economy
Standard
Premium
Deluxe

2.3   NG is deciding which of four potential venues should be used to stage an entertainment event. Demand for the event may be low, medium or high depending on weather conditions on the day. The management accountant has estimated the contribution that would be earned for each of the possible outcomes and has produced the following regret matrix:

		Regret Matrix		
Venue	Ayefield	Beefield	Ceefield	Deefield
Demand				
Low	$0	$200,000	$300,000	$450,000
Medium	$330,000	$110,000	$0	$150,000
High	$810,000	$590,000	$480,000	$0

Which venue would be chosen if the company applies the minimax regret criterion?

Select...   ▼
Ayefield
Beefield
Ceefield
Deefield

2.4 **What is meant by "budgetary slack"?**

Select... ▼
The lead time between the preparation of the functional budgets and the approval of the master budget by senior management
The difference between the budgeted output and the actual output
The difference between budgeted capacity utilisation and full capacity
The intentional over estimation of costs and/or under estimation of revenue in a budget

2.5 "xxx" describes the relationship between utilisation of resources (inputs) and the output produced by those resources.

Improving "xxx" means getting more output from each unit of input, or getting the same amount of output with fewer resources.

What does "xxx" refer to in this definition?

Select... ▼
Economy
Efficiency
Effectiveness
Value-for-money

2.6 A company manufactures two products (L and M) using the same material and labour. It holds no inventory. Information about the variable costs and maximum demands are as follows:

	Product L	Product M
	$ per unit	$ per unit
Material ($4 per litre)	13	19
Labour ($7 per hour)	35	28
	Units	Units
Maximum monthly demand	6,000	8,000

Each month 50,000 litres of material and 60,000 labour hours are available.

Which of the inputs is/are limiting factors?

Select... ▼
Material only
Labour only
Neither material nor labour
Both material and labour

(12 marks)

3 NUMBER ENTRY

3.1 X Co uses a throughput accounting system. Details of product A, per unit, are as follows:

Selling price	$320
Material costs	$80
Conversion costs	$60
Time on bottleneck resource	6 minutes

What is the return per hour for product A (to the nearest $)?

$ [   ]

3.2 Albrecht has received a request to make a special version of one of its basic products. This special version will use 2,000 units of material X.

Material X is no longer used by Albrecht but there are 2,000 units left in inventory that had been purchased at $4·00 per unit. The current purchase price is $4·75 per unit. Albrecht believes it could sell material X for $3·00 per unit. However, material X is similar to material Y that is currently in use by Albrecht and can be purchased for $6·50 per unit. It could use material X in place of material Y – however, it would cost $2·75 per unit to modify material X so that it could be used in place of material Y.

What is the relevant cost per unit of material X for the manufacture of the special version (to two decimal places)?

$ [   ]

3.3 A company makes a single product which it sells for $2 per unit.

Fixed costs are $13,000 per month.

The contribution/sales ratio is 40%.

Sales revenue is $62,500.

What is the margin of safety (to the nearest whole unit)?

[   ] units

3.4 Posquade Co produces a single product. Budgeted sales volume for the next three month periods is 50,000 units. Production capacity is 18,000 units per month. The following per unit information is available:

	$	$
Selling price		160
Variable cost	80	
Fixed overheads	33	
Total cost		113
Profit		47

A potential overseas customer has requested a price for an initial order of 3,000 units over the next three months.

What is the minimum price per unit that should be quoted (to the nearest \$) to ensure that a loss is not made on the order?

$ [   ]

3.5 You have just timed a hairdresser doing a haircut for the first time. It took 50 minutes.

What is the learning rate (to the nearest whole %) if the hairdresser took 35 minutes to do the second haircut?

[   ] %

3.6 The Northern division of Gemas Co currently earns a return on investment of 15·5%, based on capital employed of $2,680,000. The divisional management team have decided to implement a project which will require an investment of $320,000. The project is expected to generate a profit of $53,000 per annum. The Northern division's cost of capital is 13%.

What will be the residual income of the division (to the nearest \$) after the project is implemented?

$ [   ]

3.7 DB manufactures and sells e-readers. The standard labour cost per unit of the product is $7. Each unit takes 0.5 hours to produce at a labour rate of $14 per hour. The budgeted production for August was 20,000 units.

The Production Director subsequently reviewed the market conditions that had been experienced during August and determined that market labour rates were $17.50 per hour. The actual production was 22,000 units. Actual labour hours worked were 11,400 hours at $15.50 per hour.

It is the policy of the company to calculate labour rate planning variances based on actual hours paid.

What was the adverse labour rate planning variance (to the nearest \$) during August?

$ [   ]

(14 marks)

4 HOT AREA

4.1 Identify, by selecting the relevant box in the table below, whether each statement regarding life cycle costing is true or false.

It helps forecast a product's profitability over its entire life	TRUE	FALSE
It takes into account a product's total costs over its entire life	TRUE	FALSE
It focuses on the production of monthly profit statements throughout a product's entire life	TRUE	FALSE
It includes costs of product design and marketing	TRUE	FALSE

4.2 Identify, by selecting the relevant box in the table below, whether each statement regarding outsourcing is true or false.

It always leads to short-term cost savings	TRUE	FALSE
It normally reduces the risk of under-utilising the resources used in undertaking the activity internally	TRUE	FALSE
It is never used for manufacturing activities	TRUE	FALSE
It increases the risk that confidential information about the organisation's products may be passed on to competitors	TRUE	FALSE

4.3 Identify, by selecting the relevant box in the table below, whether each statement about residual income is true or false.

It is calculated by adding back depreciation and deducting the notional interest charge	TRUE	FALSE
It eliminates the effect of accounting policies from the assessment of performance	TRUE	FALSE
It assesses divisional income based on the book value of the investment which has been made	TRUE	FALSE
It does not take the risk of specific projects into account	TRUE	FALSE

4.4 Identify, by selecting the relevant box in the table below, whether each statements about transfer pricing is correct or incorrect.

Cost-based transfer prices encourage the transferring division to control costs	CORRECT	INCORRECT
A transferring division's profit can be maximised at a transfer price below market price	CORRECT	INCORRECT
Market-based transfer prices always maximise overall company profits	CORRECT	INCORRECT
Cost-based transfer prices never lead to goal incongruence	CORRECT	INCORRECT

(8 marks)

5 HOT SPOT

5.1 Four lines representing expected costs and revenue have been drawn on the break-even chart below:

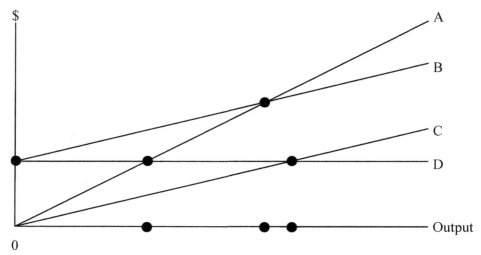

Identify the break-even volume by clicking on the point on the graph that corresponds to this.

5.2 The following graph relates to a linear programming problem:

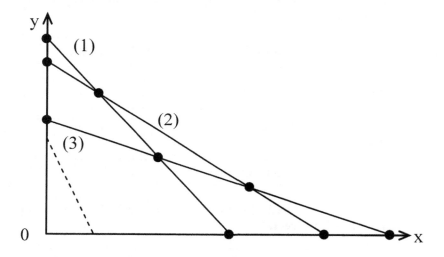

The objective is to maximise contribution and the dotted line on the graph depicts this function. There are three constraints which are all of the "less than or equal to" type which are depicted on the graph by the three solid lines labelled (1), (2) and (3).

Identify the point of maximum contribution by clicking on the graph to identify its position.

5.3 A company manufactures and sells two products (X and Y) which have contributions per unit of $8 and $20 respectively. The company aims to maximise profit. Two materials (G and H) are used in the manufacture of each product. Both materials are in short supply; only 1,000 kg of G and 1,800 kg of H are available next period. Each unit of X uses 8 kg of material G and 12 kg of material H, while each unit of product Y uses 10 kg of material G and 20 kg of material H. The company holds no inventory and it can sell all the units produced.

The management accountant has drawn the following graph accurately showing the constraints for materials G and H:

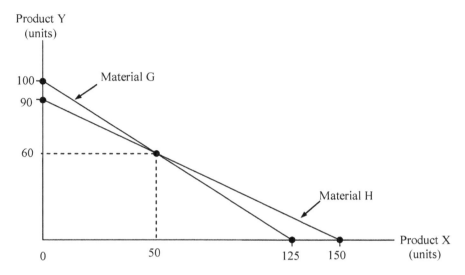

Identify the point of maximum contribution by clicking on the graph to identify its position.

5.4 Nerville makes and sells a range of three gardening products. Budgeted data for the next year is as follows:

Product	E375	F294	G142
	$	$	$
Selling price per unit	246	300	160
Variable cost per unit	126	135·	100
Contribution per unit	120	165	60
Budgeted sales volume (units)	20,000	17,000	16,000

Budgeted fixed overheads are $1,519,000.

The profit volume chart below is to be completed on the assumption that the three products are sold in their budgeted mix.

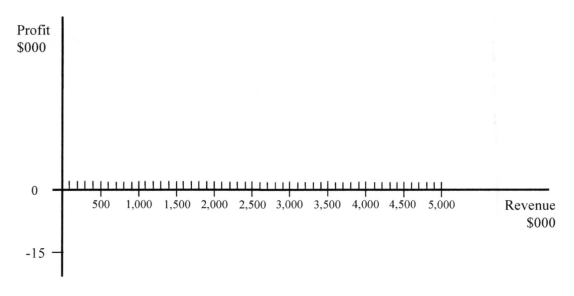

Calculate break even revenue if sales are made in the budgeted mix and click on the chart to identify its position.

(8 marks)

6 ENHANCED MATCHING

6.1 A textiles manufacturer makes three textiles at its Bigtown factory; Ax, By and Cz. The dyeing process has been identified as a bottleneck resource.

Information about the three products is as follows:

Product	Ax	By	Cz
	$	$	$
Selling price per metre	10	11	12.5
Material cost per metre	3.0	3.0	4.0
Other variable costs	2.0	3.5	2.0
Time taken in dyeing per metre	10 minutes	10 minutes	15 minutes

The manufacturer wishes to maximise throughout contribution.

Rank the textiles in order of priority for the throughput maximising production plan.

HIGH PRIORITY	
LOW PRIORITY	

Ax
By
Cz

6.2   A company produces three products, D, E and F. The statement below shows the selling price and product costs per unit for each product, based on a traditional absorption costing system:

	D	E	F
	$	$	$
Selling price per unit	32	28	22
Variable costs per unit			
Direct material	10	8	6
Direct labour	6	4	4
Variable overhead	4	2	2
Fixed cost per unit	9	6	6
Total product cost	29	20	18

Additional information:

	D	E	F
Time in process A (minutes)	20	25	15

Process A time is limited to 2,500 hours per period.

Rank the products in order of priority on the assumption that a traditional contribution approach is used in order to maximise profit?

HIGH PRIORITY	
LOW PRIORITY	

D
E
F

6.3   A company has entered two different new markets.

In market A, it is initially charging low prices so as to gain rapid market share while demand is relatively elastic.

In market B, it is initially charging high prices so as to earn maximum profits while demand is relatively inelastic.

Match the pricing policy used to each market.

Price policy	
Penetration pricing	
Price Skimming	

Market A
Market B

6.4   **Match each of the following budgeting approaches to the correct description.**

Description   Budgeting Approach

One that is set prior to the control period and not subsequently changed in response to changes in activity, costs or revenues		Flexed budget
One that is continuously updated by adding a further accounting period when the earliest accounting period has expired		Fixed budgeting
One that is changed in response to changes in the level of activity		Rolling budgeting
Is based on decision packages, where each decision package shows the costs of each proposed activity performed.		Zero based budgeting

6.5   A hospital management team assess performance using value for money.

Match each of the following performance measures to the correct element of value for money.

Performance measures   *Value for money*

Number of patients who need to be re-admitted following surgery		Economy
Staff cost of each surgical procedure		Efficiency
Number of patients per doctor		Effectiveness

6.6   **Match each of the following types of information system to the management level that is most likely to use it.**

Information system   *Management level*

Decision support systems		Strategic
Transaction processing systems		Tactical
Executive information systems		Operational

6.7 Def Co provides accounting services to government departments. On average, each staff member works six chargeable hours per day, with the rest of their working day being spent on non-chargeable administrative work. One of the company's main objectives is to produce as high level of quality and customer satisfaction.

Def Co has set a number of targets for the next year.

Indicate which of these targets assesses economy, efficiency and effectiveness at Def Co.

Economy	Efficiency	Effectiveness

Targets		
(1)	Cutting departmental expenditure by 5%	
(2)	Increasing the number of chargeable hours handled by advisers to 6.2 per day	
(3)	Obtaining a score of 4.7 or above on customer satisfaction surveys	

(14 marks)

OT CASES

Question 1 YAM CO

The following scenario relates to questions 1–5.

Yam Co is involved in the processing of sheet metal into products A, B and C using three processes, pressing, stretching and rolling.

Information about the three products (per metre) is as follows:

	Product A	Product B	Product C
	$	$	$
Selling price	70.0	60.0	70.0
Variable costs:			
Materials	3.0	2.5	10.0
Labour	10.0	10.0	15.0

Other factory costs are all fixed and total $17,975,000 per year.

Raw material for the sheet metal is first pressed then stretched and finally rolled. The pressing process has been identified as the bottleneck and the factory manager has provided the following data:

	Pressing time per metre		
	Product A	Product B	Product C
Hours	0.50	0.50	0.40

There are 225,000 hours of pressing time available each year.

Maximum demand for each product is 200,000 metres per year.

1   **How many metres of each product should be made per year in order to maximise profit?**

	Product A	Product B	Product C
A	200,000	200,000	25,000
B	200,000	200,000	200,000
C	200,000	90,000	200,000
D	450,000	0	0

2   The finance director has just told you that the company has employed sufficient labour to work 700,000 hours per year, which is sufficient to meet maximum demand. Labour is paid $10 per hour. Due to agreements with the unions, Yam Co is committed to paying for this amount of labour in full.

Match each product to the order in which it should be manufactured to ensure that throughput contribution is maximised.

Produce first			Product A
Produce second			Product B
Produce third			Product C

3   The throughput return per factory hour for Product C has been calculated as $150.

What is the throughput accounting ratio for Product C, to two decimal places?

☐

4   Yam Co also makes a fourth product, product D. Product D has a throughput accounting ratio of less than one and the management accountant has stated that under no circumstances should product D be made.

Which of the following statements regarding ceasing production of Product D are correct?

Many of the fixed costs relating to Product D may not be avoided even if production is ceased	TRUE	FALSE
Demand for other products may be adversely affected by ceasing production of Product D	TRUE	FALSE
The throughput accounting ratio of product D could be improved by increasing the time spent on the bottleneck resource	TRUE	FALSE
It may be possible to increase the selling price of product D and this would increase the throughput accounting ratio	TRUE	FALSE

5   **Which of the following statements about the Theory of Constraints is/are true?**

It is essential that labour idle time on non-bottleneck resources is minimised	TRUE	FALSE
Throughput is maximised by reducing the impact of bottlenecks	TRUE	FALSE

(10 marks)

Question 2 STOW HOTEL

The following scenario relates to questions 1–5.

The managers of Stow Hotel are trying to decide on their pricing strategy for the next financial year. Occupancy levels depend on the price charged, and the managers are trying to decide between charging $180, $200 or $220 per day.

The variable costs of running the hotel are uncertain, due to fluctuation in the prices of food and energy. Costs may be high, most likely or low. The management accountant has produced a profit table (payoff matrix) summarising the possible levels of contribution for each price charged:

	Client fee per day		
State of variable cost	$180	$200	$220
	$	$	$
High	1,339	1,378	1,313
Most likely	1,496	1,509	1,418
Low	1,733	1,706	1,575

1   **Match the fee that should be chosen under the maximax and maximin decision rules.**

Decision rule		Fee
Maximax		$180
Maximin		$200
		$220

2   The probabilities of variable cost levels occurring at the high, most likely and low levels are estimated as 0·1, 0·6 and 0·3 respectively.

         What are the expected values of contribution for each fee strategy?

	$180	$200	$220
A	1,496	1,509	1,418
B	1,551	1,555	1,455
C	1,522	1,531	1,435
D	1,473	1,489	1,402

3   The management accountant started to calculate a "table of regrets" but did not complete it. The table is missing the regrets for the low level of variable costs:

		Client fee per day strategy		
State of variable cost		$180	$200	$220
High		39	0	65
Most likely		13	0	91
Low		?	?	?

         What are regrets for each fee strategy for the low level of variable costs?

	$180	$200	$220
A	394	328	262
B	0	27	131
C	27	0	131
D	0	27	158

4   The management of Stow Hotel are risk seekers.

         Which decision making technique is appropriate for risk seekers?

Select... ▾
Expected values
Maximin
Maximax
Minimax regret

5 **Identify, by selecting the relevant box in the table below, whether each of the following statements regarding the use of expected values for decision making are correct or incorrect?**

They accurately reflect the risks associated with each decision	CORRECT	INCORRECT
They are more appropriate for actions that will be repeated many times	CORRECT	INCORRECT
They may be unreliable as the probabilities used are estimates	CORRECT	INCORRECT
They are used by risk neutral decision makers	CORRECT	INCORRECT

(10 marks)

Question 3 EASYAIR

The following scenario relates to questions 1–5.

Easyair Co was founded seven years ago, and is one of a growing number of low-cost airlines in the country of Shania. Summarised financial information for the most recent financial year is provided below:

	$m
Operating profit	700
Interest payable	(100)
Profit before tax	600
Tax	(200)
Profit after tax	400
Statement of financial position extracts	
Non-current liabilities	300
Share capital	100
Retained earnings	2,000

1 **What was the return on capital employed for the year (to the nearest %)?**

[   ] %

2 The asset turnover ratio has been calculated as 1.9 times.

What is the operating profit margin (to the nearest %)?

[   ] %

3   Easyair Co had a cash balance of $100 million at the end of the year. The finance director believes that this should have been used to repay some of the non-current liabilities on the last day of the year. However, this was not done, and the financial statements above reflect the fact that the liability was not repaid.

What impact would repaying the non-current liabilities on the last day of the financial year have had on the following financial ratios?

Return on capital employed	INCREASE	NO IMPACT
Return on equity	INCREASE	NO IMPACT

4   Easyair Co is considering introducing the "balanced scorecard" to allow the airline to monitor performance effectively.

Which THREE of the following are advantages of using the balanced scorecard for monitoring performance?

☐   It aims to measure a wider range of aspects of performance rather than just focussing on financial aspects

☐   Performance measures are linked to objectives which are based on the organisation's strategy

☐   If focusses management's attention on value for money objectives

☐   It measures the organisation's performance from the perspective of a wide range of stakeholders

☐   It contains a small number of key performance indicators, ensuring than senior management focus on the important areas of the business

5   **Which FOUR of the following are perspectives of the balanced scorecard?**

☐   Financial

☐   Competitiveness

☐   Customer

☐   Resource utilisation

☐   Internal business

☐   Flexibility

☐   Quality

☐   Learning and growth

(10 marks)

Question 4 MOBE CO

The following scenario relates to questions 1–5.

Mobe Co manufactures electronic mobility scooters. The company is split into two divisions: the scooter division (Division S) and the motor division (Division M). Division M supplies electronic motors to both Division S and to external customers. The two divisions run as autonomous profit centres; Division M has the freedom to decide how many motors to sell to Division S and how many to sell to external customers, and Division S may buy motors externally or from Division M. Details of the two divisions are given below:

Division S

Division S's budget for the coming year shows that 35,000 electronic motors will be needed. An external supplier could supply these to Division S for $800 each.

Division M

Division M has the capacity to produce a total of 60,000 electronic motors per year. Details of Division M's budget, which has just been prepared for the forthcoming year, are as follows:

Budgeted sales volume (units)	60,000
Selling price per unit for external sales of motors	$850
Variable costs per unit for external sales of motors	$770

The variable cost per unit for motors sold to Division S is $30 per unit lower due to cost savings on distribution and packaging.

Maximum external demand for the motors is 35,000 units per year.

1   **If the transfer price for the motors is set at $760 per motor how many motors per year will Division M be willing to sell to Division S?**

         ☐ Units

2   **How many motors should Division M supply to Division S in order to maximise group profits?**

         ☐ Units

3   Head office has now introduced a new policy stating that Division M must sell 35,000 motors per year to Division S. It wants Division M to set a total price for all 35,000 motors.

     What is the minimum total transfer price at which Division M would be willing to sell 35,000 motors to Division S?

     $ ☐

4   **Which THREE of the following are objectives of a good transfer pricing system?**

☐   To ensure that decisions taken by divisional managers are in the interests of the organisation as a whole

☐   To assist managers in budget preparation

☐   To give divisional managers autonomy in making decisions about trading with other divisions

☐   To encourage divisions within an organisation to trade with each other rather than buying or selling externally

☐   To allow a fair measure of divisional performance

5   **Which TWO of the following statements about the use of the "full cost plus" method of setting transfer prices are correct?**

☐   It always ensures that the supplying division is compensated for the opportunity cost of lost contribution on external sales

☐   It motivates the supplying division to keep costs under control

☐   The transfer price covers the costs of production of the supplying division if actual output exceeds budgeted output

☐   It may lead to dysfunctional decisions if the supplying division has spare capacity

(10 marks)

OBJECTIVE TEST ANSWERS

1   MULTIPLE RESPONSE

1.1

☑   Activity based costing

☑   Life-cycle costing

☑   Input output analysis

1.2

☑   The product mix ratio

☑   Contribution to sales ratio for each product

☑   General fixed costs

1.3

☑   Average time to settle insurance claims

☑   Percentage of policy renewals

Tutorial note: *New insurance products would come within the learning and growth perspective, as would spending on training.*

1.4

☑   Materials usage variances

☑   Percentage of products that are defective after inspection

Tutorial note: *Tom has responsibility for production, which implies cost, but not for revenue. Therefore any measures that include profit would not be appropriate for measuring Tom's performance.*

1.5

☑   It enables comparison of performance of divisions which are not of common size

☑   It does not take account of the risk of project investments being undertaken

☑   Managers will be encouraged to invest in projects with higher returns

Tutorial note: *ROI* **can** *lead to goal incongruent decisions. For example, where a manager rejects a project because it yields a lower ROI than the manager's existing ROI, even if the project's return exceeds the company's hurdle ROI.*

1.6

☑   Some additional costs are incurred on external sales

☑   The selling division has some spare capacity after satisfying external demand for its output

1.7

☑ The reliability of expected value calculations is heavily influenced by the accuracy of the probabilities assigned to outcomes

☑ Expected values take account of the risk associated with a decision

1.8

☑ Generation of revenues

☑ Investment in working capital

Tutorial note: *The manager of a profit centre does not have control over investment in non-current assets and hence has no control over depreciation expense. Investment in working capital is determined by the non-current assets and liabilities that arise from revenues generated and associated costs incurred by the profit centre, so this is controllable.*

2   PULL-DOWN LIST

2.1   This is the objective of **target costing**.

2.2   Since only three products can be made, the **Deluxe** would be dropped:

Per unit	Economy	Standard	Premium	Deluxe
Selling price	$28	$32	$37	$40
Variable cost	$13	$16	$20	$22
Contribution per unit	15	16	17	18
Direct labour hours per unit	0·17	0·22	0·28	0·31
Contribution per labour hour	88.24	72.72	60.71	58.06
⇒ ranking	1st	2nd	3rd	4th

2.3   **Deefield**

Maximum regret if Ayefield venue is chosen is $ 810,000
Maximum regret if Beefield venue is chosen is $ 590,000
Maximum regret if Ceefield venue is chosen is $ 480,000
Maximum regret if Deefield venue is chosen is $ 450,000

Deefield has the lowest maximum regret, so would be chosen.

2.4   **The intentional over estimation of costs and/or under estimation of revenue in a budget.**

2.5   **Efficiency**

Economy focuses on cost per unit of input not on outputs per unit of input, so is not correct. Effectiveness looks at how well the organisation provides the service it aims to produce. Value for money covers all "3Es". **Efficiency** is the correct answer.

2.6 **Both material and labour**

Material required to meet maximum demand:
$6,000 \times (13 \div 4) + 8,000 \times (19 \div 4) =$ 57,500 litres
Material available: 50,000 litres
So material is a limiting factor
Labour required to meet maximum demand:
$6,000 \times (35 \div 7) + 8,000 \times (28 \div 7) =$ 62,000 hours
Labour available: 60,000 hours
So labour is a limiting factor

3   NUMBER ENTRY

3.1 $(\$320 - \$80) \div (6 \div 60) = \$ \boxed{2400}$

Tutorial note: *Commas are not accepted in number entry questions, so the answer is 2400 and not 2,400.*

3.2   The relevant cost of material X is the opportunity cost as it is not used regularly. There are two options regarding material X:

Option 1 – sell it for $3.00 per unit.

Option 2 – use as substitute for material Y. Relevant cost is the saving per kg unit of material Y ($6.5) less the cost of modifying each unit of material X so it can be used in place of Y ($2.75) = $ $\boxed{3.75}$

Option 2 has the higher benefit, so this is what Albrecht would do with the 2,000 units of material X if they are not used on the contract. This is therefore the opportunity cost.

3.3   Sales = $62,500
Break even sales = $13,000 ÷ 0·4 = $32,500
Margin of safety (sales revenue) = $30,000

Margin of safety (units) $30,000 ÷ $2 = $\boxed{15000}$ units.

3.4 $ $\boxed{80}$ The minimum price is the relevant cost. Capacity is 54,000 per quarter (18,000 × 3). Domestic sales are 50,000 per quarter – so there is spare capacity of 4,000 units per quarter. The potential order from the overseas customer can be satisfied without any loss of domestic sales so there is no opportunity cost. The relevant cost is therefore the incremental cost, which is the variable cost per unit.

3.5   Cumulative average for two times = ½ (50 + 35) = 42.5

$\Rightarrow$ as cumulative output doubles (from 1 to 2 units) cumulative average time fell to $\boxed{85}$ % (42.5 ÷ 50).

3.6

	$	$
Capital employed before project	2,680,000	
Current profit (ROI of 15·5%)		415,400
Profit from project		53,000
Profit including project		468,400
Investment in project	320,000	
Capital employed after project	3,000,000	
Imputed cost of capital at 13%		390,000
Residual income		**78400**

3.7

	$
Actual hours at original standard rate (11,400 × 14)	159,600
Actual hours at revised standard rate (11,400 × 17.5)	199,500
Labour planning rate variance	39,900

$ **39900**

4 HOT AREA

4.1

It helps forecast a product's profitability over its entire life	**TRUE**	
It takes into account a product's total costs over its entire life	**TRUE**	
It focuses on the production of monthly profit statements throughout a product's entire life		**FALSE**
It includes costs of product design and marketing	**TRUE**	

4.2

It always leads to short-term cost savings		**FALSE**
It normally reduces the risk of under-utilising the resources used in undertaking the activity internally	**TRUE**	
It is never used for manufacturing activities		**FALSE**
It increases the risk that confidential information about the organisation's products may be passed on to competitors	**TRUE**	

4.3

It is calculated by adding back depreciation and deducting the notional interest charge		**FALSE**
It eliminates the effect of accounting policies from the assessment of performance		**FALSE**
It assesses divisional income based on the book value of the investment which has been made	**TRUE**	
It does not take the risk of specific projects into account		**FALSE**

4.4

Cost-based transfer prices encourage the transferring division to control costs (1)		**INCORRECT**
A transferring division's profit can be maximised at a transfer price below market price (2)	**CORRECT**	
Market-based transfer prices always maximise overall company profits (3)		**INCORRECT**
Cost-based transfer prices never lead to goal incongruence (4)		**INCORRECT**

Tutorial note: *(1) is incorrect – if the transfer price is based on actual cost, all costs are passed on by the transferring division, so it will have no incentive to reduce them. (2) is correct – the transferring division may be able to supply another internal division at a lower cost than selling externally, so a transfer price below market price could still maximise profits. (3) is incorrect – market-based transfer prices can lead to decisions which are goal incongruent (e.g. if the buying division cannot make a profit if it buys from the transferring division at market price, so no transfer takes place, even though the profits of the company overall might be increased). Similarly, (4) is incorrect as a cost-based transfer price may be too high or too low and so lead to decisions that do not maximise the overall profits of the organisation (i.e. not goal congruent).*

5   HOT SPOT

5.1

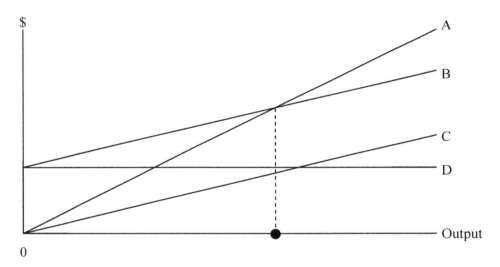

Tutorial note: *Line A shows total revenue; Line B total costs. Where these two lines intersect is the break-even point.*

5.2

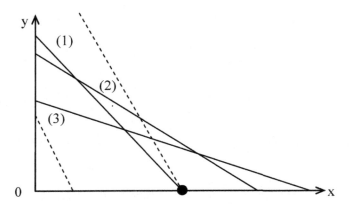

Tutorial note: *Additional contribution lines can be drawn on the graph. Each contribution line represents a particular level of contribution, and will be parallel to the contribution line drawn on the graph in the question. A second contribution line has been added above – this represents the highest value of contribution that can be obtained within the feasible region, at the point where line (1) crosses the X axis.*

5.3

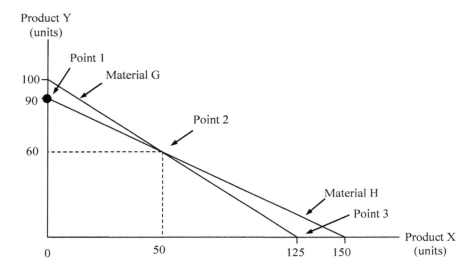

Tutorial note: *The point of maximum contribution will be one of the three intersection points Calculating contribution at each point gives:*

Point 1

90 units of Y, 0 units of X ⇒ contribution = 1,800 (90 × $20)

Point 2

50 units of X and 60 units of Y
Contribution = 1,600 (50 × 8 + 60 × 20).

Point 3

125 unit of Y, 0 units of X ⇒ Contribution = $1,000 (125 × 8)

Contribution is therefore maximised at point 1, where 90 units of Y and 0 units of X are produced.

5.4

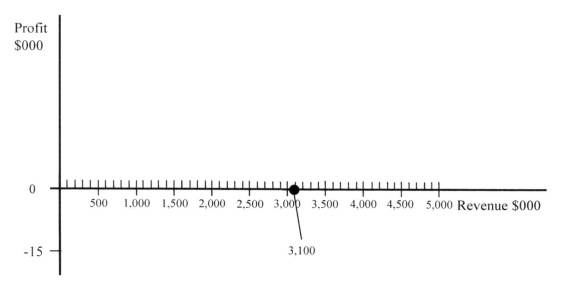

Workings

Product	E375	F294	G142	Total
Selling price per unit	246	300	160	
Budgeted sales volume (units)	20,000	17,000	16,000	
⇒ budgeted revenue ($000)	4,920	5,100	2,560	12,580
Contribution per unit	120	165	60	
⇒ budgeted contribution ($000)	2,400	2,805	960	6,165

$$\Rightarrow \text{weighted average C/S ratio} = \frac{6{,}165}{12{,}660} = 0.49$$

$$\text{Break even revenue} = \frac{\text{Budgeted fixed cost}}{\text{C/S ratio}} = \frac{1{,}519{,}000}{0.49} = 3{,}100{,}000.$$

6   ENHANCED MATCHING

6.1

HIGH PRIORITY	By
	Ax
LOW PRIORITY	Cz

WORKING

Product	Ax	By	Cz
Selling price per metre	10	11	12.5
Material cost per metre	3.0	3.0	4.0
Throughput contribution per metre	7	8	8.5
Time taken in dyeing (minutes)	10	10	15
Metres per hour	6	6	4
Throughput contribution per hour	42	48	34
Therefore ranking	②	①	③

6.2

HIGH PRIORITY	F
	D
LOW PRIORITY	E

WORKING

	D	E	F
Contribution per unit	$12	$14	$10
Units of limiting factor (minutes)	20	25	15
Contribution per unit of limiting factor	$0.60	$0.56	$0.667
Ranking	2nd	3rd	1st

6.3

Price policy	Market
Penetration pricing	Market A
Price Skimming	Market B

6.4

Description	Budgeting Approach
One that is set prior to the control period and not subsequently changed in response to changes in activity, costs or revenues	Fixed budgeting
One that is continuously updated by adding a further accounting period when the earliest accounting period has expired	Rolling budgeting
One that is changed in response to changes in the level of activity	Flexed budget
Is based on decision packages, where each decision package shows the costs of each proposed activity performed.	Zero based budgeting

6.5

Performance measures	Value for money
Number of patients who need to be re-admitted following surgery	Effectiveness
Staff cost of each surgical procedure	Economy
Number of patients per doctor	Efficiency

6.6

System	Management level
Decision support systems	Tactical
Transaction processing systems	Operational
Executive information systems	Strategic

6.7

Targets		Element assessed
(1)	Cutting departmental expenditure by 5%	Economy
(2)	Increasing the number of chargeable hours handled by advisors to 6.2 per day	Efficiency
(3)	Obtaining a score of 4.7 or above on customer satisfaction surveys	Effectiveness

OT CASES

Answer 1 YAM CO

Item	Answer	Justification
1	C	Decision should be based on maximising contribution per hour of scarce resource:

	Product A	Product B	Product C
Selling price	70	60	70
Raw materials	3	2.5	10
Labour	10	10.0	15
Contribution per unit	57	47.5	45
Pressing time per unit	0.5	0.5	0.4
Throughput contribution per hour of pressing time	114	95	112.5
$\Rightarrow$ Ranking	1st	3rd	2nd

Production plan – given 225,000 hours per year

	Hours
Produce 200,000 metres of Product A (max demand)	100,000
Product 200,000 metres of Product C (max demand)	80,000
$\Rightarrow$ Product 90,000 metres of Product B (with remaining hours)	45,000
	225,000

2   B

Produce first	Product C
Produce second	Product A
Produce third	Product B

WORKING

Decision should be based on throughout return per hour of scarce resource

	Product A	Product B	Product C
Selling price	70	60	70
Raw materials	3	2.5	10
Throughput contribution per unit	67	57.5	60
Pressing time per unit	0.5	0.5	0.4
Throughput contribution per hour Of pressing time	134	115	150
$\Rightarrow$ Ranking	2nd	3rd	1st

3   Throughput accounting ratio = $\dfrac{\text{Return per hour}}{\text{Factory cost per hour}} = \dfrac{\$150}{111(W)} = \boxed{\textbf{1.35}}$

WORKING

Total fixed costs are $17,975,000 plus the labour cost. Labour costs $10 per hour for each of the 700,000 hours, a cost of $7,000,000.

Total fixed cost is therefore $24,975,000

Fixed cost per bottleneck (pressing) hour is $24,975,000 ÷ 225,000 = $111 per hour.

4

Many of the fixed costs relating to Product D may not be avoided even if production is ceased	**TRUE**	
Demand for other products may be adversely affected by ceasing production of Product D	**TRUE**	
The throughput accounting ratio of product D could be improved by increasing the time spent on the bottleneck resource		**FALSE**
It may be possible to increase the selling price of product D and this would increase the throughput accounting ratio	**TRUE**	

5

It is essential that labour idle time on non-bottleneck resources is minimised		**FALSE**
Throughput is maximised by reducing the impact of bottlenecks	**TRUE**	

Tutorial note: *The first statement is correct – the majority of the costs are already included in the organisation's accounting system – however, they are often hidden within other overheads, so management are not aware of them. The second statement is incorrect because input/output analysis does not divide material flows into three categories described. It is flow cost accounting that does this. Statement 3 is incorrect – environmental management accounting information is primarily aimed at internal management.*

Answer 2 STOW HOTEL

Item   Answer   Justification

1

Decision rule	Fee
Maximax	$180
Maximin	$200

Tutorial note: *A fee of $180 gives the highest potential return, so would be chosen under maximax. The minimum returns for each fess strategy are:$1,339 for $180, $1,378 for $200 and $1,313 for $220. A fee of $200 therefore has the highest minimum return, so would be chosen under maximin.*

2   B   Expected value for each fee strategy is calculated by multiplying each potential outcome by its probability and summing these:

$180: (1,339 × 0.1) + (1,496 × 0.6) + (1,733 × 0.3) = $1,551
$200: (1,378 × 0.1) + (1,509 × 0.6) + (1,706 × 0.3) = $1,555
$220: (1,313 × 0.1) + (1,418 × 0.6) + (1,575 × 0.3) = $1,455

3   D   For the low level of variable costs, the best fee strategy would be to charge $180 as this has the highest contribution of $1,733. The regret for $180 is therefore zero.

The regret for the other two decisions is the difference between the contribution that they generate at the low level of variable cost and $1,733:

For fee strategy $200, regret is: (1,733 – 1,706) = 27
For fee strategy $220 regret is (1,733 – 1,575) = 158

4   **Maximax** is used by risk seekers

Tutorial note: *Maximin is used by risk averse decision makers (people who do not like risk). Minimax regret is also used by risk averse decision makers. Expected values are used by risk neutral decision makers.*

5

They accurately reflect the risks associated with each decision		**INCORRECT**
They are more appropriate for decisions that are repeated many times	**CORRECT**	
They may be unreliable as the probabilities used are estimates	**CORRECT**	
They are used by risk neutral decision makers	**CORRECT**	

Answer 3 EASYAIR

Item   *Answer*   *Justification*

1   $\text{ROCE} = \dfrac{\text{Operating profit}}{\text{Equity + long term liabilities}} \times 100 = \dfrac{700}{2{,}400} \times 100 = \boxed{29}\ \%$

2   B $\text{Asset turnover} = \dfrac{\text{Revenue}}{\text{Equity + long term liabilities}} = 1.9 \text{ times}$

$\Rightarrow \dfrac{\text{Revenue}}{2{,}400} = 1.9 \Rightarrow \text{Revenue} = 4560.$

$\text{Operating profit margin} = \dfrac{\text{Operating profit}}{\text{Revenue}} \times 100 = \dfrac{700}{4{,}560} \times 100 = 15.35\%$

i.e. $\boxed{15}\ \%$

3

Return on capital employed	INCREASE	
Return on equity		NO IMPACT

Justification

$\text{Return on equity} = \dfrac{\text{Profit before (or after) tax}}{\text{Equity}}$

If the liabilities were repaid on the last day of the year, there would be no impact on profit before or after tax, as the interest expense would still be due in respect of the year.

Repaying the liability would reduce cash (an asset) and reduce a liability by the same amount, but would have no impact on equity

$\Rightarrow$ No impact on return on equity.

Tutorial note: *Return on equity can be calculated as either profit before or profit after tax. Different analysts use different conventions. The important thing to remember is that it should always be stated after deducting the interest expense.*

$\text{ROCE} = \dfrac{\text{Operating profit}}{\text{Equity + long - term liabilities}}$

Repaying the non-current (i.e. long-term) liabilities would reduce capital employed but would not affect profit. The ratio would therefore increase.

4

☑   It aims to measure a wider range of aspects of performance rather than just focussing on financial aspects

☑   Performance measures are linked to objectives which are based on the organisation's strategy

☑   It contains a small number of key performance indicators, ensuring than senior management focus on the important areas of the business

Tutorial note: *One of the criticisms on the balances scorecard is that it only considers the interests of two stakeholder groups – shareholders and customers. The interests of other stakeholders such as employees and suppliers are largely ignored.*

5

☑   Financial

☑   Customer

☑   Internal business perspective

☑   Learning and Growth

Answer 4 MOBE CO

Item   *Answer*   *Justification*

1 | **25000** | Units

Division M will only be willing to sell to Division S if the transfer price exceeds marginal cost, plus the opportunity cost.

Division M has capacity to produce 60,000 motors. External demand is 35,000 per year, so division M has spare capacity of 25,000 units.

⇒ Up to 25,000 units division M would be prepared to sell for anything above marginal cost of $740 ($770 less cost savings of $30).

For additional units, there will be an opportunity cost equal to the lost contribution on external sales of $80 (850 – 770). Division M would only be prepared to sell for a price above $820 (740 + 80). (Another way of looking at this is to consider that the supplying division could sell externally for $850, so would accept an adjusted price of $820 for units sold to Division S.) This is above the transfer price of $760 so Division M would not be prepared to sell any additional units.

⇒ Division M would be prepared to sell 25,000 units to division S at a price of $760.

2 | **25000** | Units

For every motor sold externally, Division M generates contribution of $80 ($850 – $770) for the group as a whole. For every motor which Division S has to buy from outside of the group, there is an incremental cost of $60 per unit ($800 – [$770 – $30]). Therefore, from a group perspective, as many external sales should be made as possible before any internal sales are made.

Division M's total capacity is 60,000 units. Given that it can make external sales of 35,000, 35,000 units should be sold externally. The remaining 25,000 units of Division M's capacity can be used to supply Division S.

3    $ | **27110000** |

First 25,000 units can be produced from Division M's spare capacity, therefore the minimum transfer price that division M will accept will be the marginal cost of producing these, which is $740 per unit.

The minimum transfer price of the next 10,000 units equals the marginal cost plus the contribution on lost external sales, which is $820 per unit (740 + 80).

In total therefore, the minimum transfer price for 35,000 units would be $27,110,000 (740 × 25,000) + (820 × 10,000)

4

☑   To ensure that decisions taken by divisional managers are in the interests of the organisation as a whole

☑   To give divisional managers autonomy in making decisions about trading with other divisions

☑   To allow a fair measure of divisional performance

5

☑   The transfer price covers the costs of production of the supplying division if actual output exceeds budgeted output

☑   It may lead to dysfunctional decisions if the supplying division has spare capacity

ABOUT BECKER PROFESSIONAL EDUCATION

Becker Professional Education provides a single destination for candidates and professionals looking to advance their careers and achieve success in:

- Accounting

- International Financial Reporting

- Project Management

- Continuing Professional Education

- Healthcare

For more information on how Becker Professional Education can support you in your career, visit www.becker.com.

Substantially derived from content reviewed by ACCA's examining team

BECKER
PROFESSIONAL EDUCATION®

9 781785 663628